HAL LEONARD easy piano

CLASSICS

arranged by

BILL BOYD

T0066057

HAL•LEONARD CORPORATION

7777 W. BLUEMOUND RD. P.O. BOX 13819 MILWAUKEE, WI 53213

Copyright © 1986 HAL LEONARD PUBLISHING CORPORATION
International Copyright Secured   ALL RIGHTS RESERVED   Printed in the U.S.A.
Unauthorized copying, arranging, adapting, recording or public performance is an infringement of copyright
Infringers are liable under the law

BARCAROLLE

By JACQUES OFFENBACH

Copyright © 1986 HAL LEONARD PUBLISHING CORPORATION
International Copyright Secured   ALL RIGHTS RESERVED   Printed in the U.S.A.

3

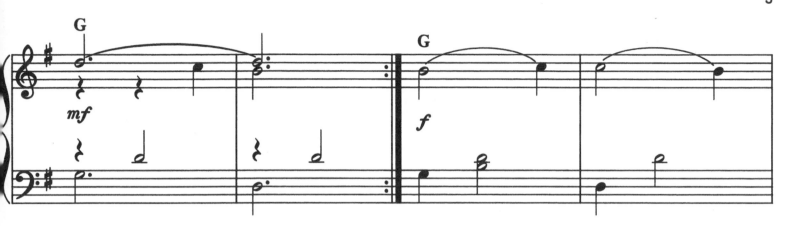

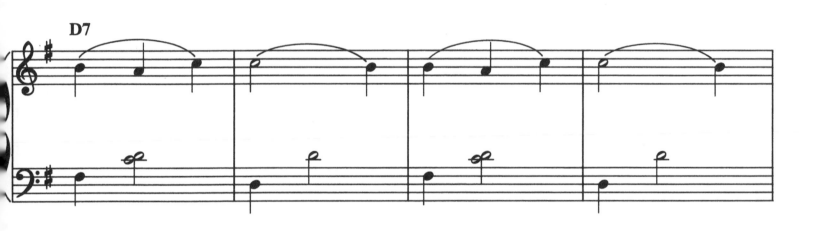

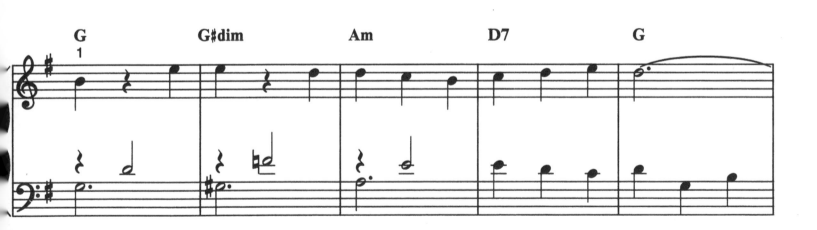

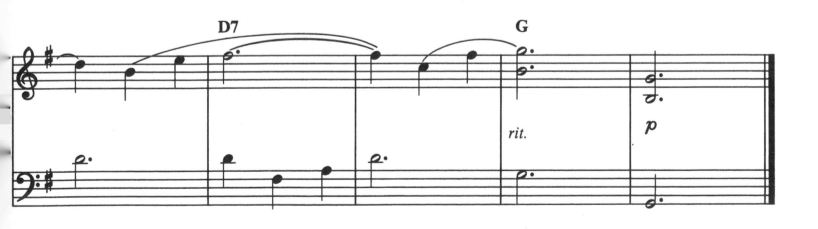

CLAIR DE LUNE

By CLAUDE DEBUSSY

Copyright © 1986 HAL LEONARD PUBLISHING CORPORATION
International Copyright Secured   ALL RIGHTS RESERVED   Printed in the U.S.A.

EINE KLEINE NACHTMUSIK

(2nd mvt.)

By WOLFGANG AMADEUS MOZART

Copyright © 1986 HAL LEONARD PUBLISHING CORPORATION
International Copyright Secured   ALL RIGHTS RESERVED   Printed in the U.S.A.

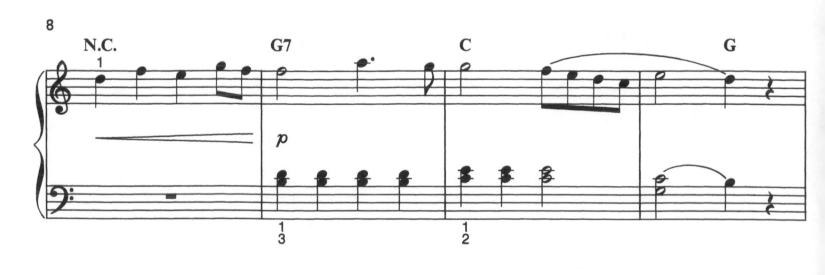

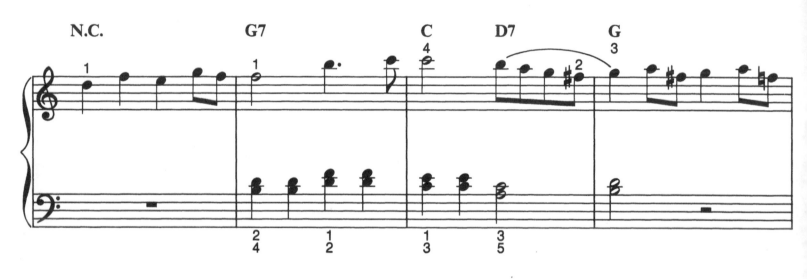

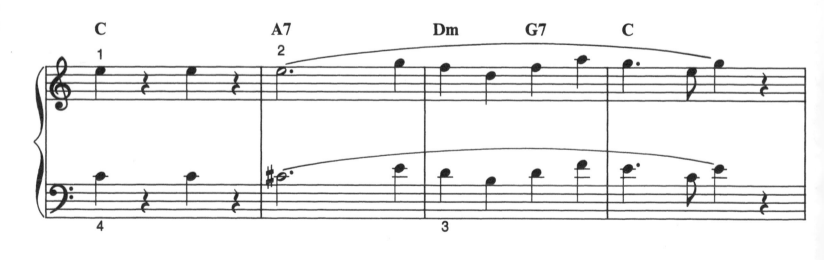

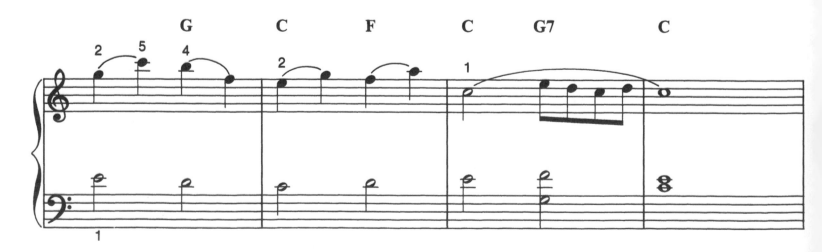

"EMPEROR" WALTZ

By JOHANN STRAUSS

Copyright © 1986 HAL LEONARD PUBLISHING CORPORATION
International Copyright Secured   ALL RIGHTS RESERVED   Printed in the U.S.A.

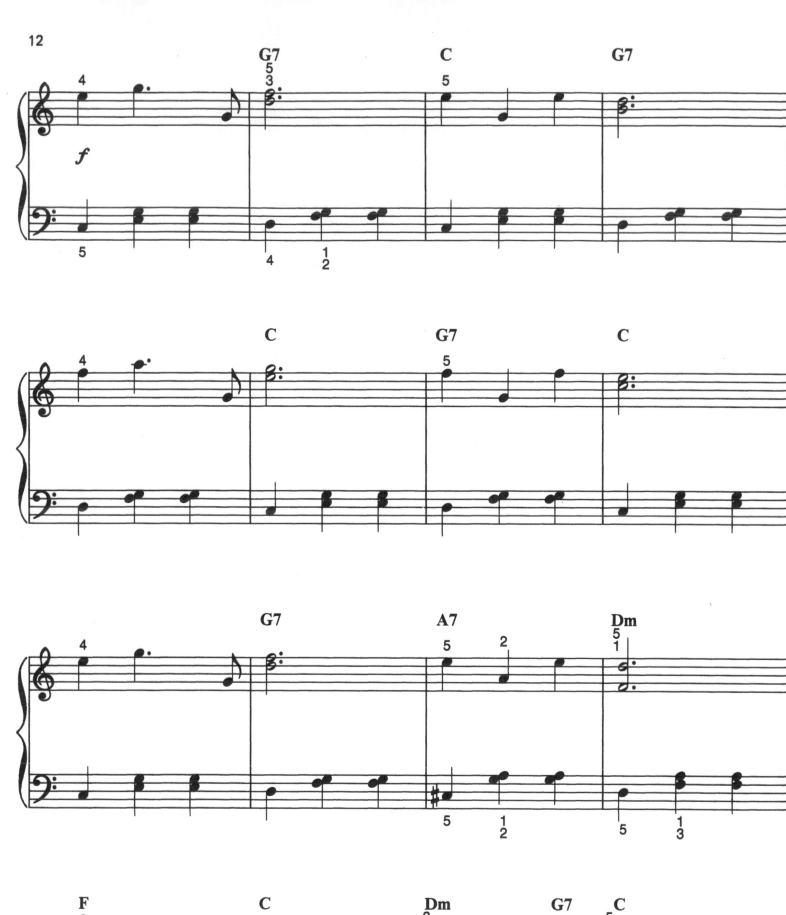

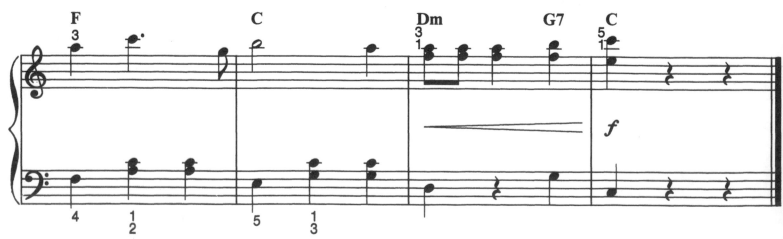

FIFTH SYMPHONY

(1st mvt.)

LUDWIG VAN BEETHOVEN

Copyright © 1986 HAL LEONARD PUBLISHING CORPORATION
International Copyright Secured   ALL RIGHTS RESERVED   Printed in the U.S.A

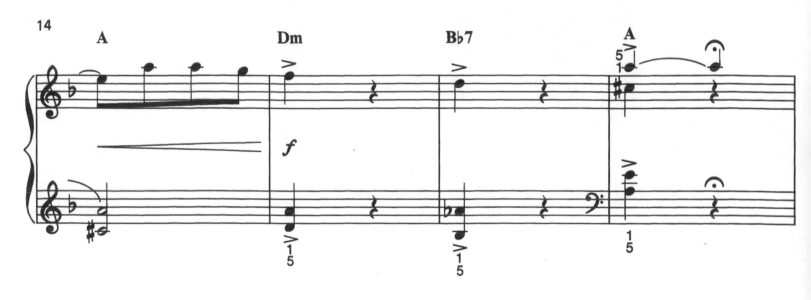

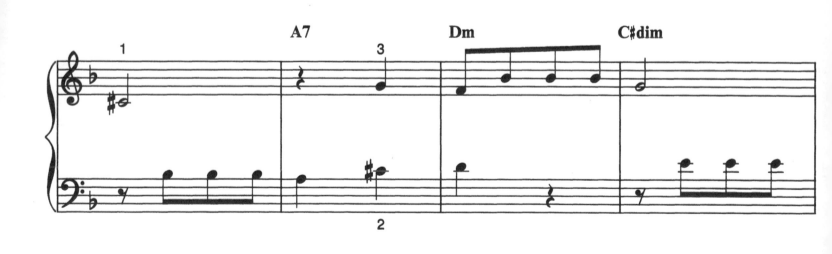

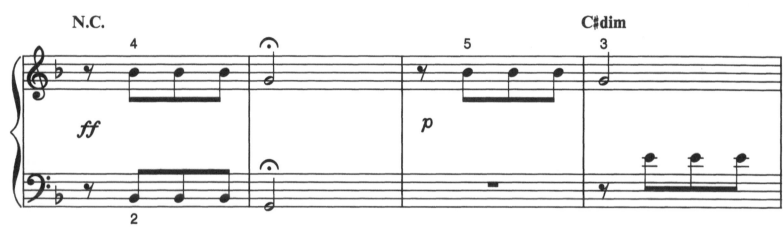

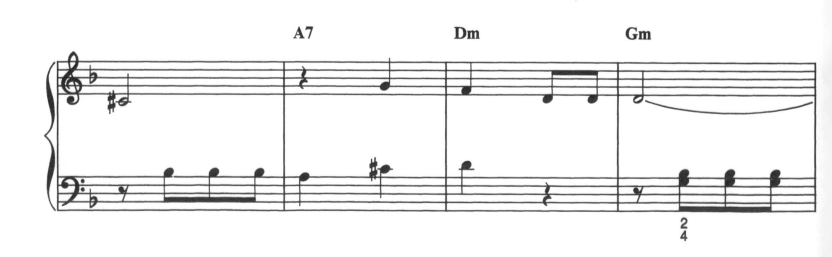

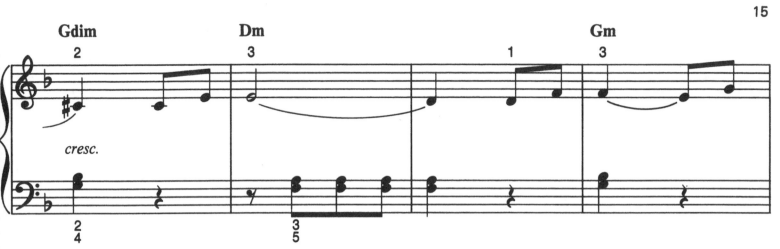

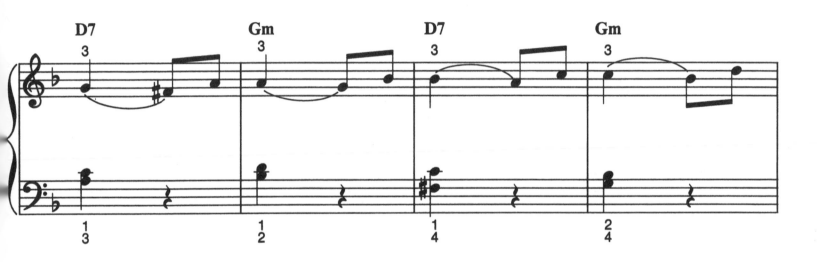

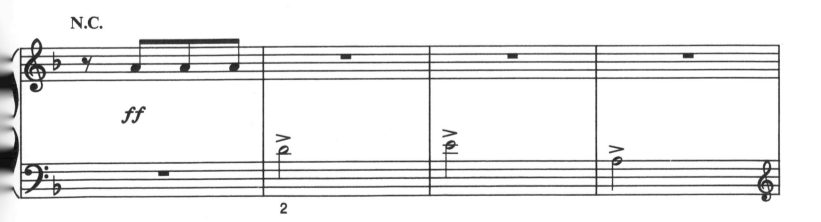

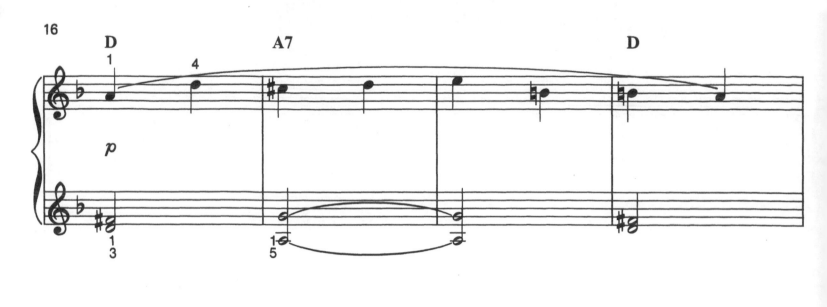

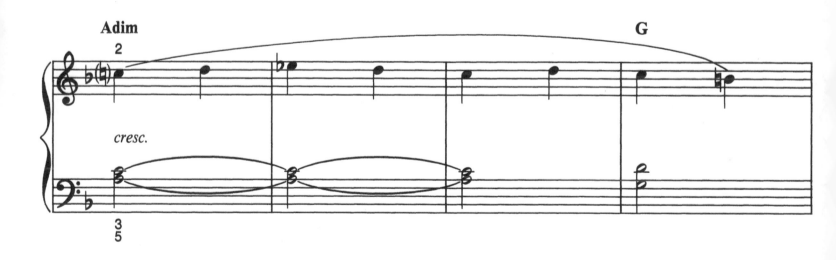

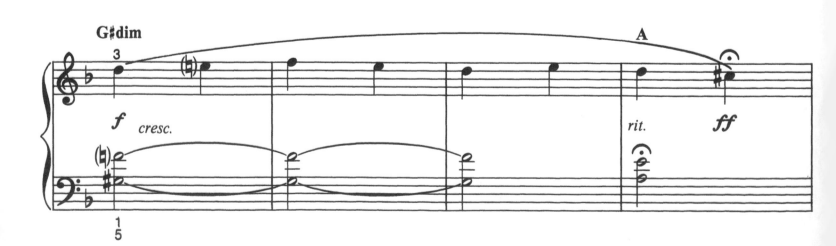

FANTAISIE-IMPROMPTU

By FREDERIC CHOPIN

Copyright © 1986 HAL LEONARD PUBLISHING CORPORATION
International Copyright Secured   ALL RIGHTS RESERVED   Printed in the U.S.A.

FIFTH SYMPHONY
(1st mvt.)

By FRANZ SCHUBERT

Copyright © 1986 HAL LEONARD PUBLISHING CORPORATION
International Copyright Secured   ALL RIGHTS RESERVED   Printed in the U.S.A

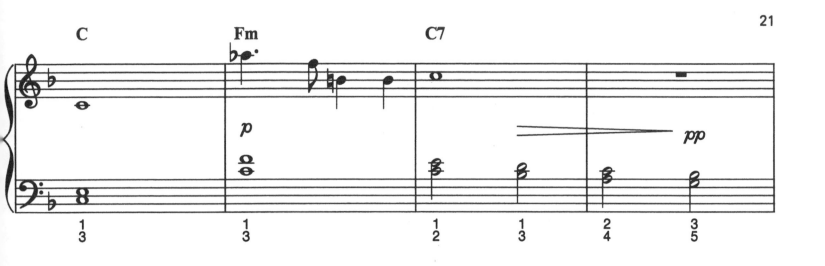

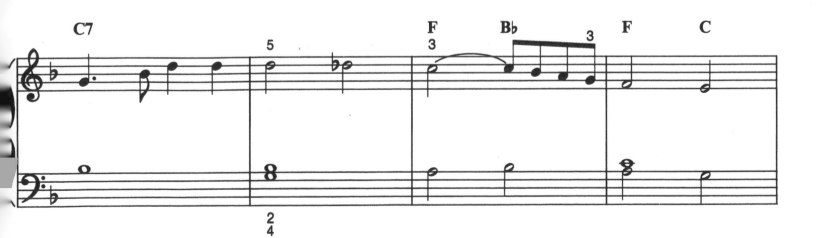

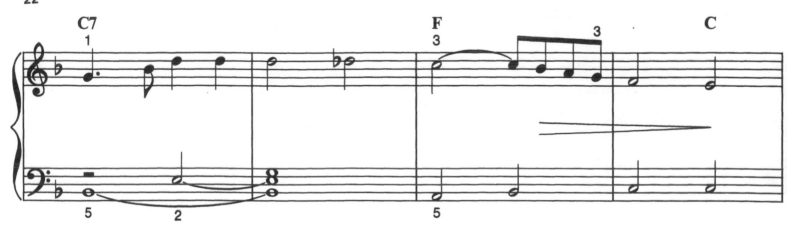

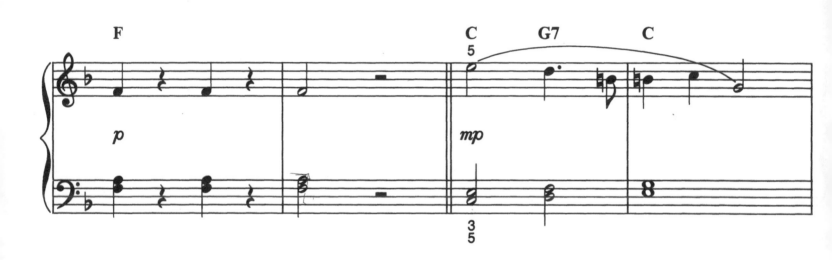

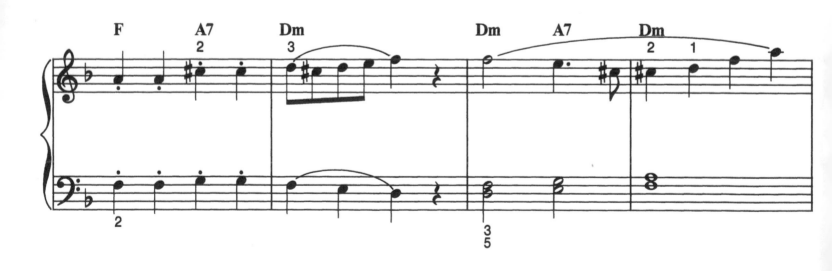

FUNERAL MARCH
OF A MARIONETTE

By CHARLES GOUNOD

Copyright © 1986 HAL LEONARD PUBLISHING CORPORATION
International Copyright Secured   ALL RIGHTS RESERVED   Printed in the U.S.A.

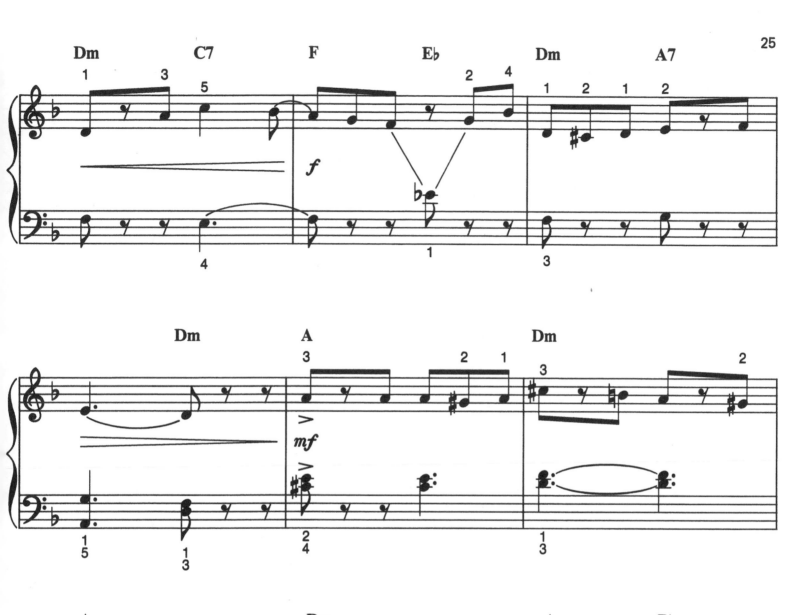

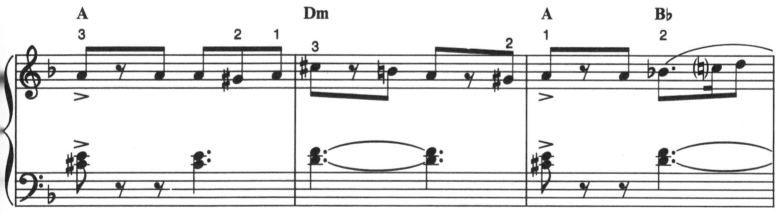

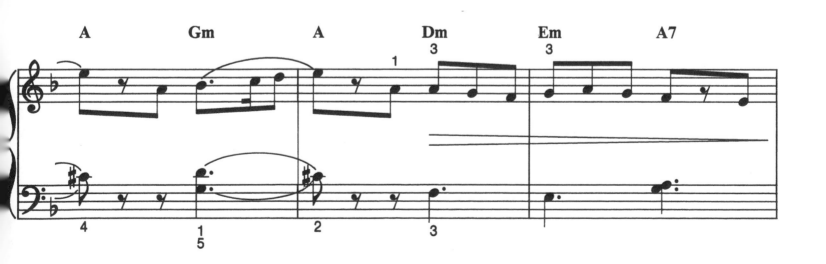

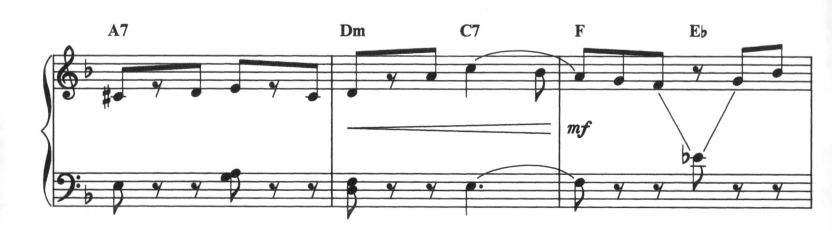

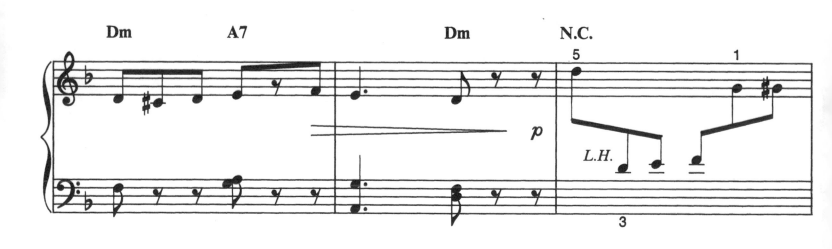

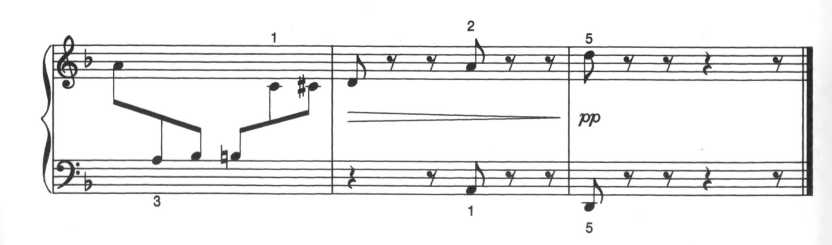

JESU, JOY OF MAN'S DESIRING

Slowly and evenly

By JOHANN SEBASTIAN BACH

Copyright © 1986 HAL LEONARD PUBLISHING CORPORATION
International Copyright Secured   ALL RIGHTS RESERVED   Printed in the U S A

FÜR ELISE

By LUDWIG VAN BEETHOVEN

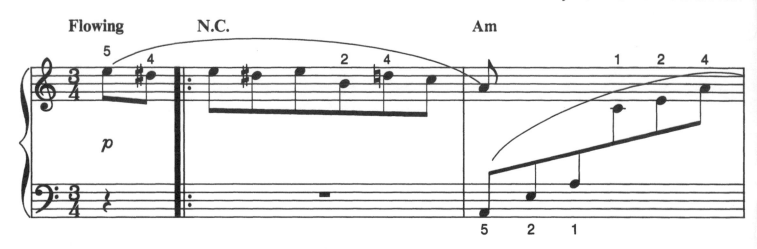

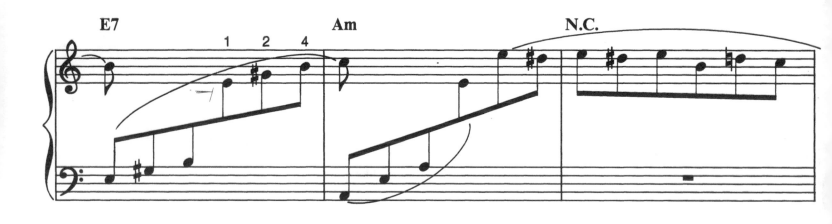

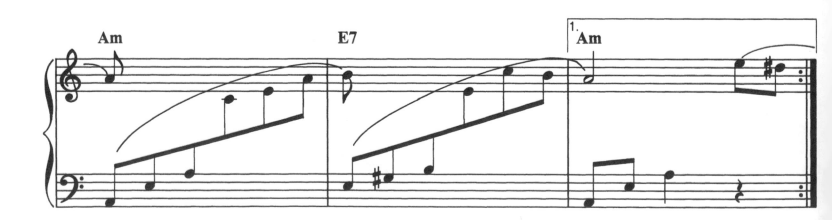

Copyright © 1986 HAL LEONARD PUBLISHING CORPORATION
International Copyright Secured   ALL RIGHTS RESERVED   Printed in the U S A.

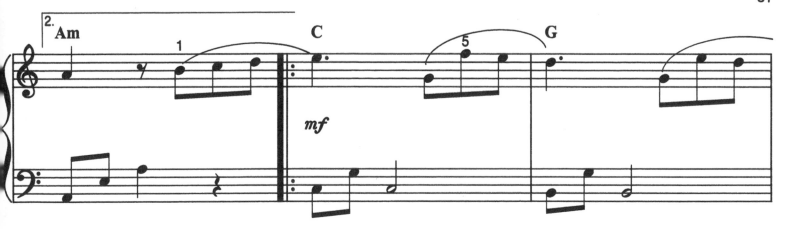

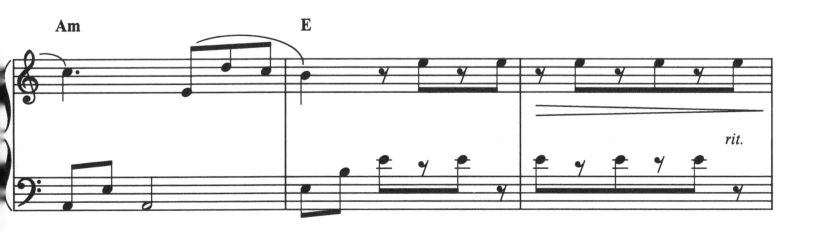

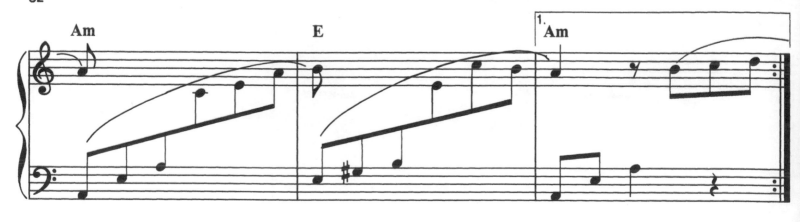

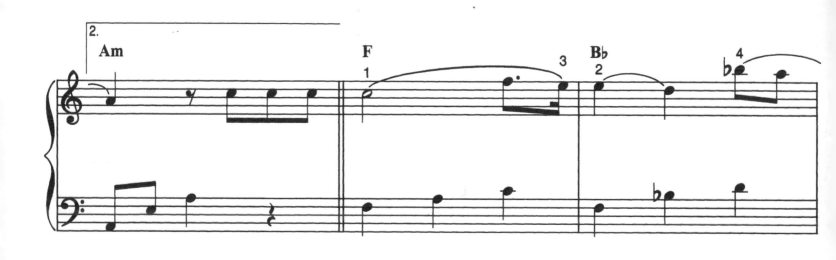

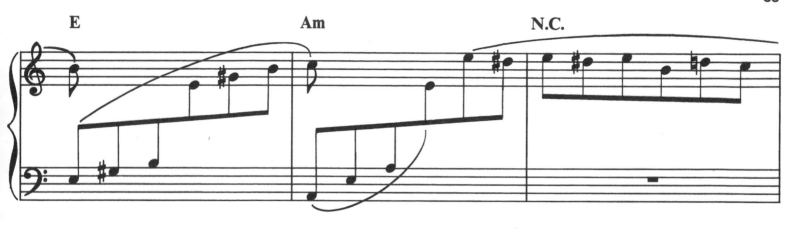

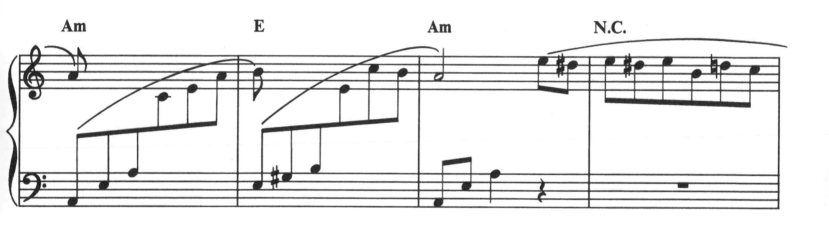

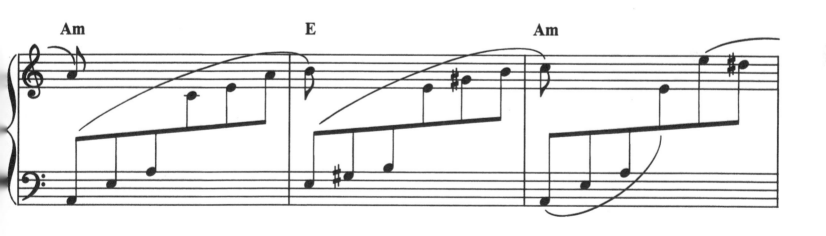

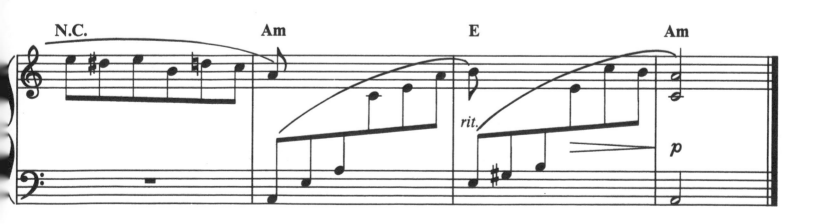

LARGO

By ANTONIN DVOŘÁK

Slowly

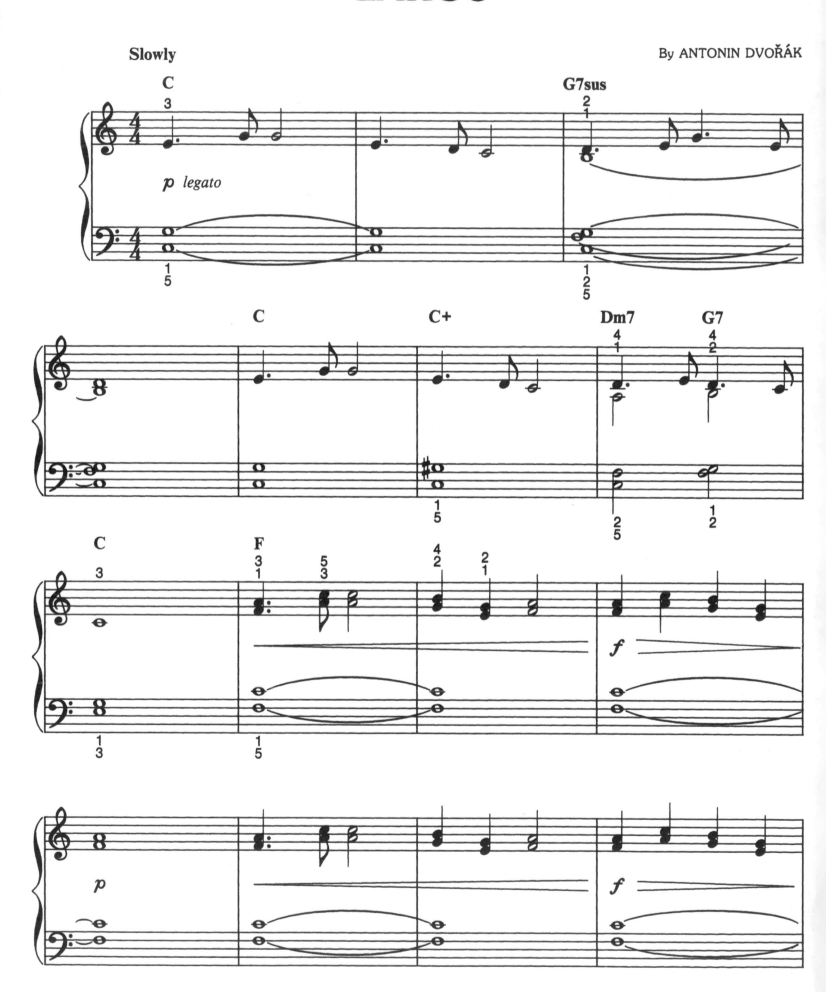

Copyright © 1986 HAL LEONARD PUBLISHING CORPORATION
International Copyright Secured   ALL RIGHTS RESERVED   Printed in the U.S.A.

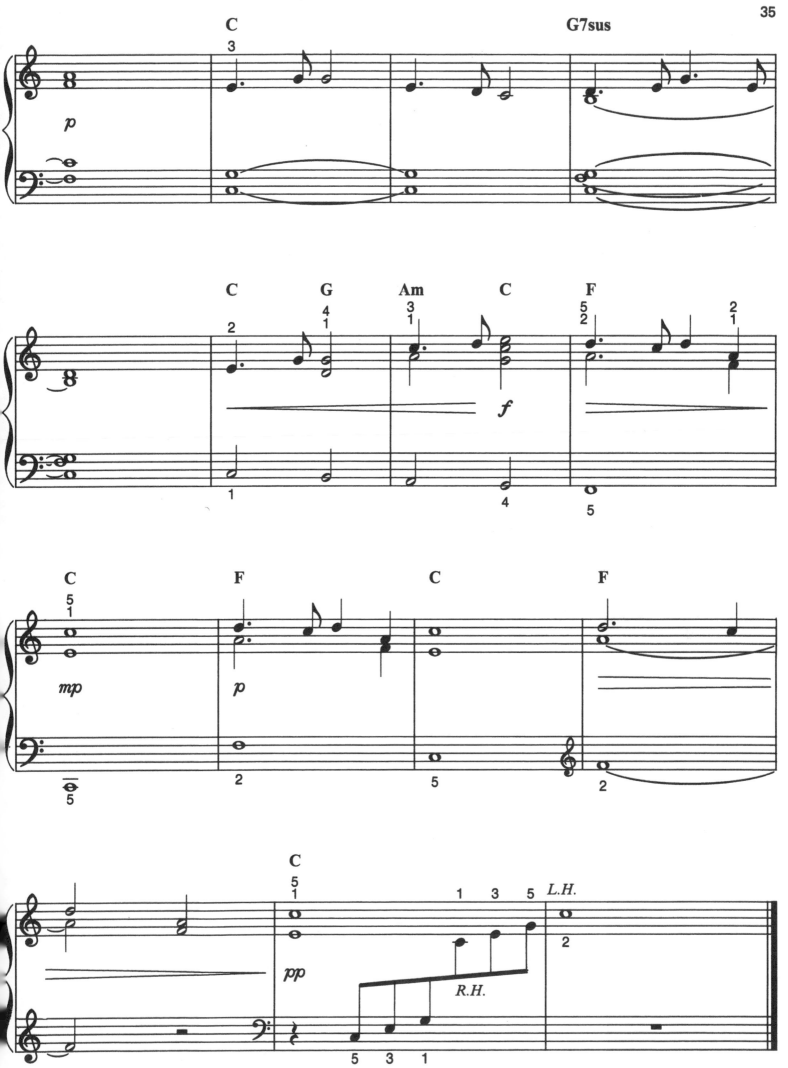

MINUET IN G

By JOHANN SEBASTIAN BACH

Copyright © 1986 HAL LEONARD PUBLISHING CORPORATION
International Copyright Secured   ALL RIGHTS RESERVED   Printed in the U.S.A.

"MOONLIGHT" SONATA

(1st mvt.)

By LUDWIG VAN BEETHOVEN

Copyright © 1986 HAL LEONARD PUBLISHING CORPORATION
International Copyright Secured   ALL RIGHTS RESERVED   Printed in the U S A

PRELUDE

By FREDERIC CHOPIN
Op. 28, No. 7

Original Key A Major

Copyright © 1986 HAL LEONARD PUBLISHING CORPORATION
International Copyright Secured   ALL RIGHTS RESERVED   Printed in the U.S.A

PIANO SONATA

(K. 331; 1st mvt.)

By WOLFGANG AMADEUS MOZART

Copyright © 1986 HAL LEONARD PUBLISHING CORPORATION
International Copyright Secured   ALL RIGHTS RESERVED   Printed in the U.S.A.

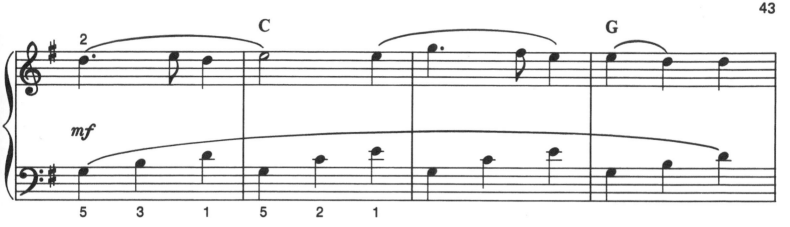

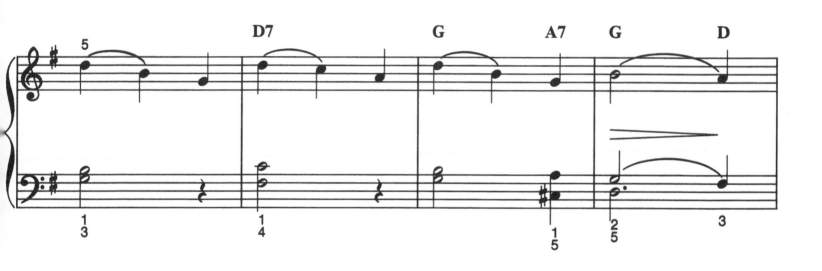

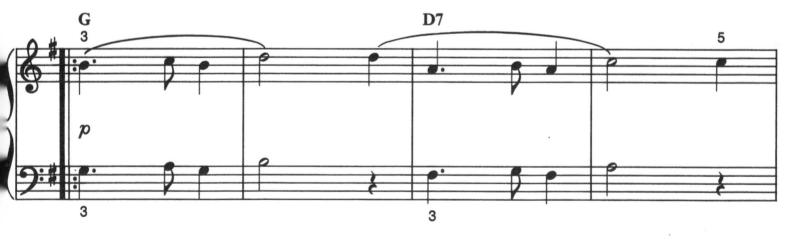

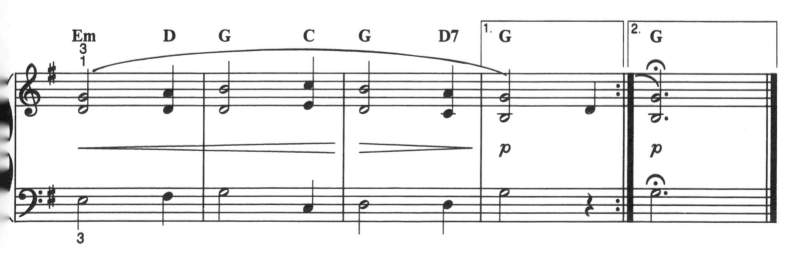

PRELUDE IN C

(Well-Tempered Clavier vol. 1)

By JOHANN SEBASTIAN BACH

Copyright © 1986 HAL LEONARD PUBLISHING CORPORATION
International Copyright Secured   ALL RIGHTS RESERVED   Printed in the U.S.A.

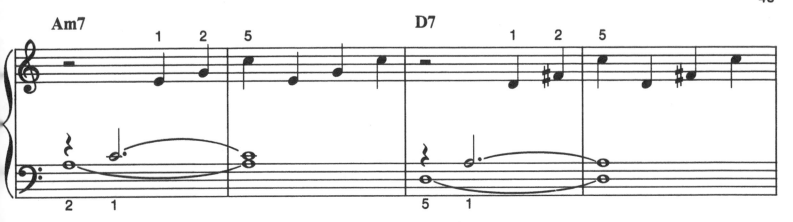

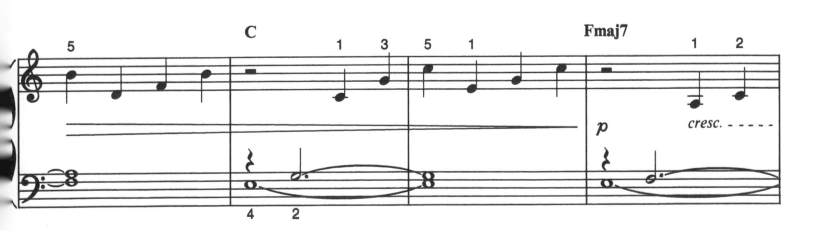

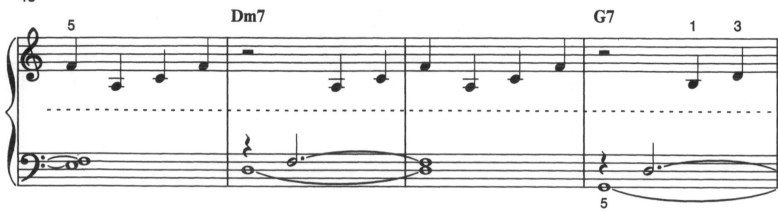

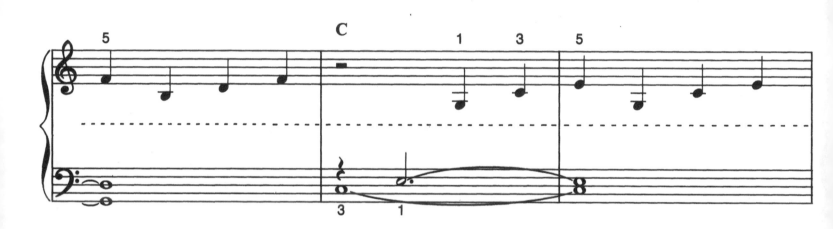

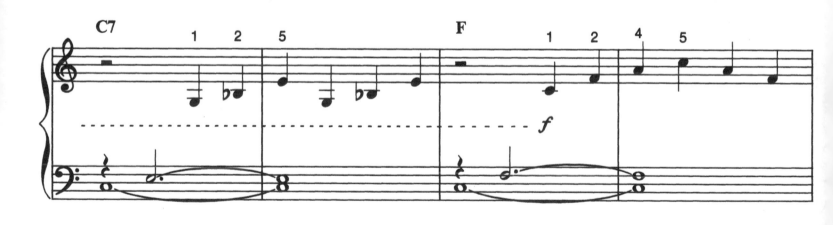

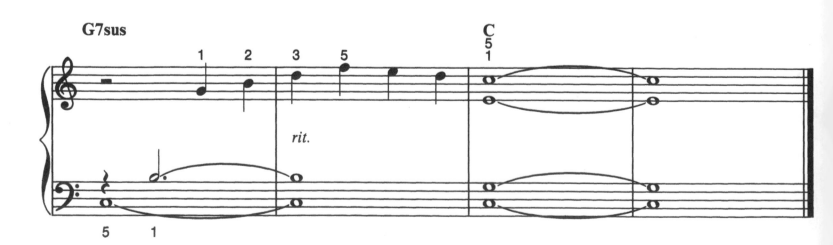

SPINNING SONG

By ALBERT ELLMENREICH

Copyright © 1986 HAL LEONARD PUBLISHING CORPORATION
International Copyright Secured   ALL RIGHTS RESERVED   Printed in the U.S.A

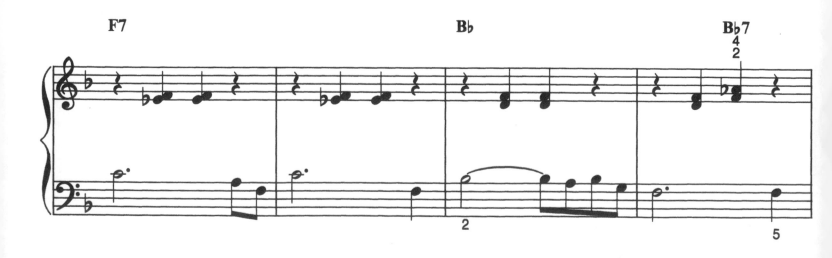

PRELUDE

By FREDERIC CHOPIN
Op. 28, No. 20

Slowly in 2

Ped. each beat

p

Original Key C Minor

Copyright © 1986 HAL LEONARD PUBLISHING CORPORATION
International Copyright Secured   ALL RIGHTS RESERVED   Printed in the U.S.A.

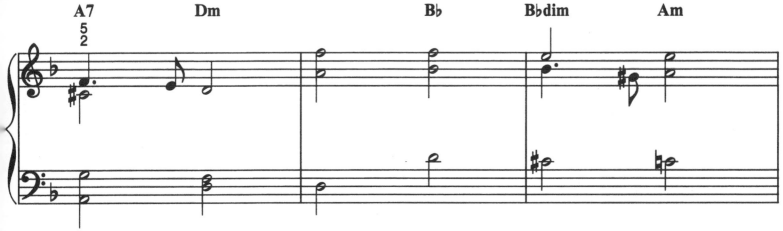

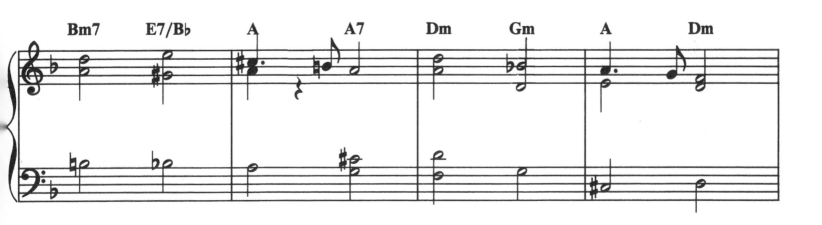

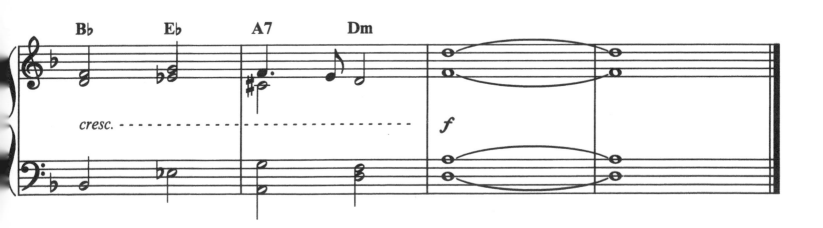

TO A WILD ROSE

By EDWARD MacDOWELL

Copyright © 1986 HAL LEONARD PUBLISHING CORPORATION
International Copyright Secured   ALL RIGHTS RESERVED   Printed in the U.S.A.

VIOLIN CONCERTO
(3rd mvt.)

By LUDWIG VAN BEETHOVEN

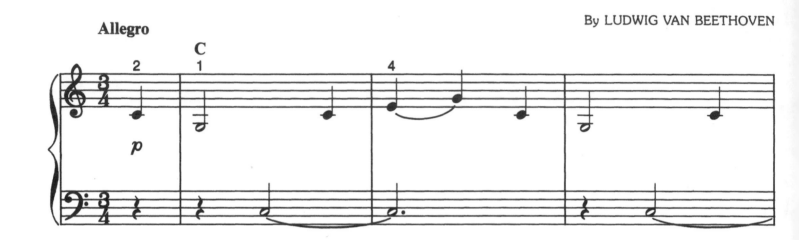

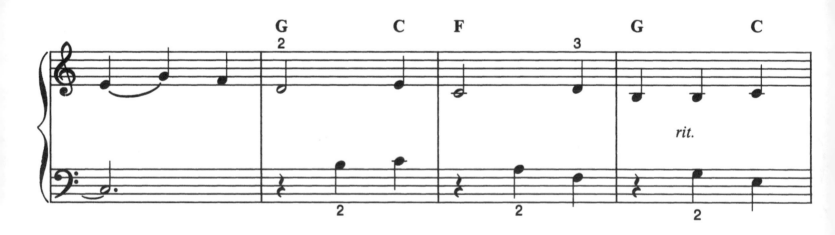

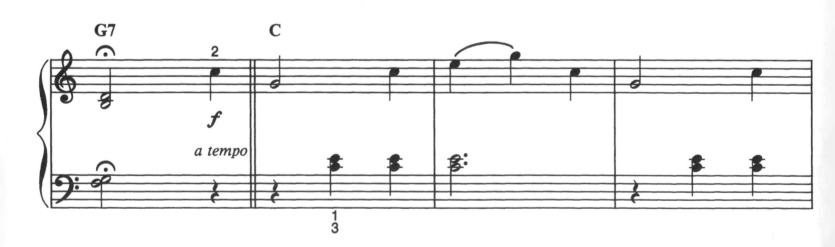

Copyright © 1986 HAL LEONARD PUBLISHING CORPORATION
International Copyright Secured   ALL RIGHTS RESERVED   Printed in the U.S.A.

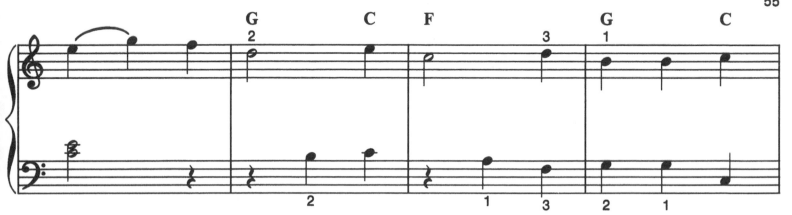

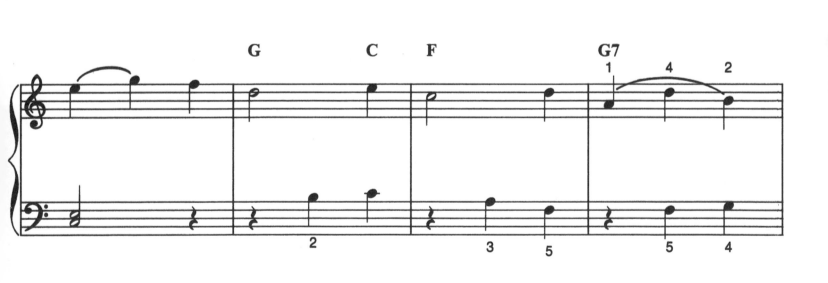

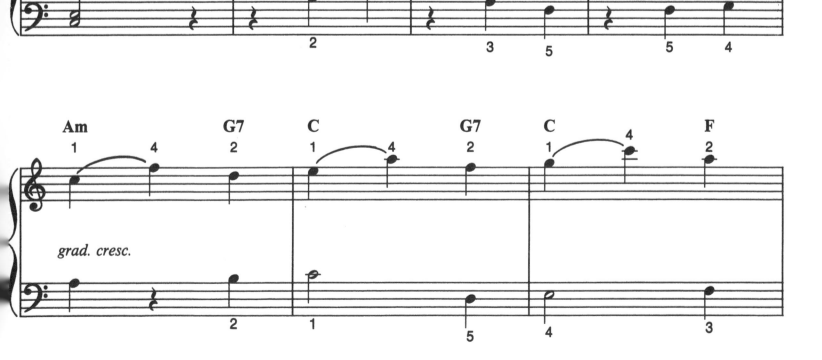

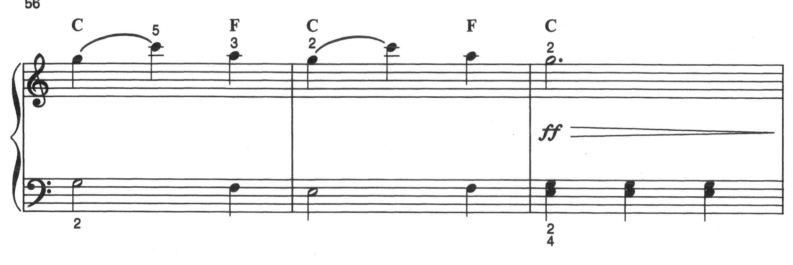

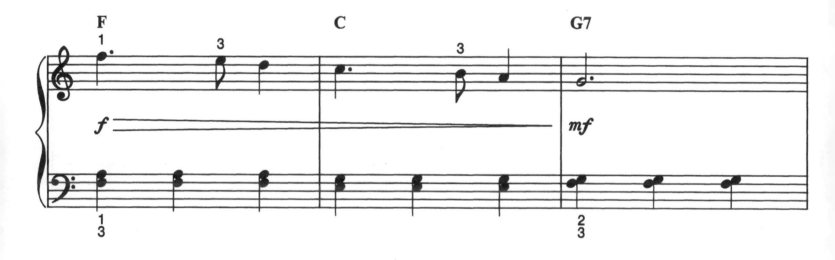

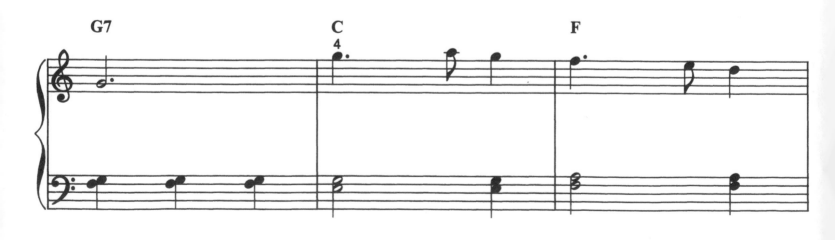

WILD HORSEMAN

By ROBERT SCHUMANN

Copyright © 1986 HAL LEONARD PUBLISHING CORPORATION
International Copyright Secured   ALL RIGHTS RESERVED   Printed in the U.S.A.

"WILLIAM TELL" Overture

(opening theme: "Morning")

By GIOACCHINO ROSSINI

Copyright © 1986 HAL LEONARD PUBLISHING CORPORATION
International Copyright Secured   ALL RIGHTS RESERVED   Printed in the U.S.A.

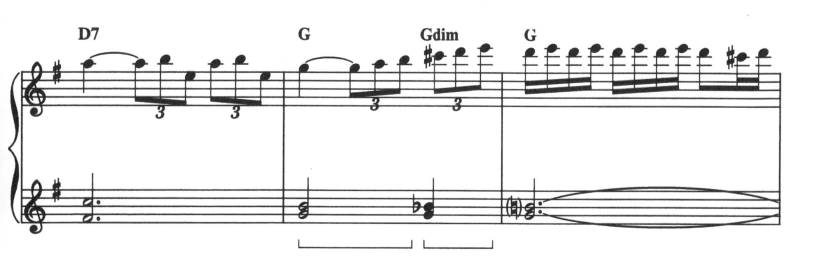

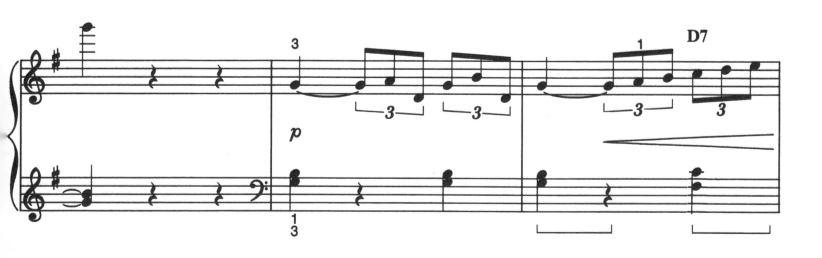

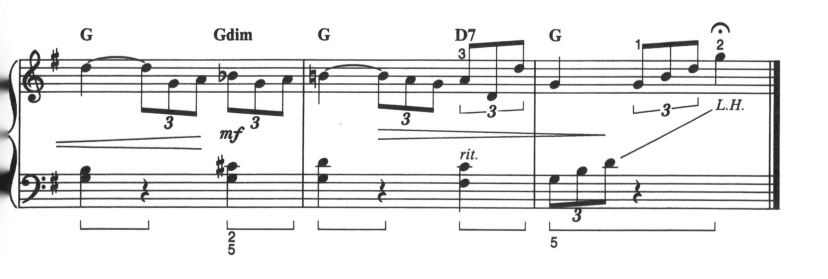

TOCCATA IN D MINOR

Copyright © 1986 HAL LEONARD PUBLISHING CORPORATION
International Copyright Secured   ALL RIGHTS RESERVED   Printed in the U.S.A.

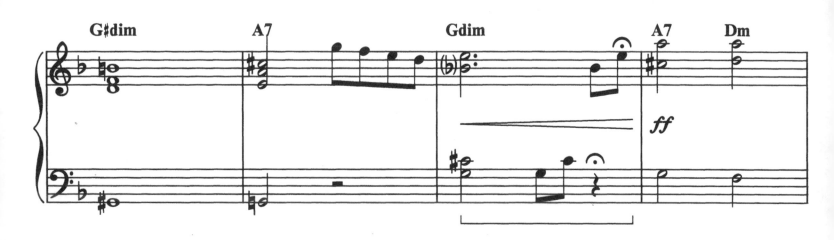

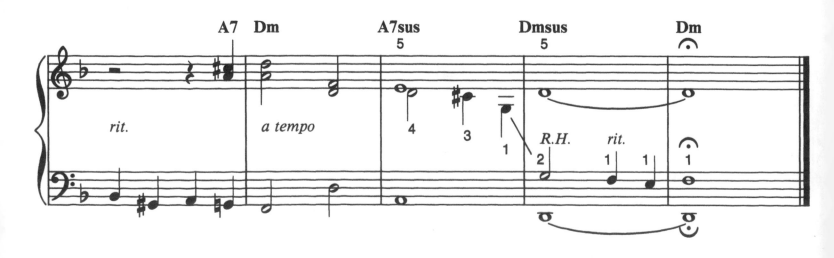